My Naughty Little Sister at the Fair

Dorothy Edwards &
Shirley Hughes

METHUEN CHILDREN'S BOOKS
London

A long time ago, when I was a little girl, I had a sister who was very much younger than me. Although my sister was often naughty, most of the naughty things she did were so funny that no one was cross with her for very long and she made a lot of friends.

Here is a story about one of my sister's adventures. It is called My Naughty Little Sister At The Fair.

When I was a little girl, my little sister used to eat all her breakfast up, and all her dinner up, and all her tea up, and all her supper up – every bit.

But one day my naughty little sister wouldn't eat her breakfast. She had cornflakes and an egg, and a piece of bread and butter, and an apple, and a big cup of milk, and she wouldn't eat anything.

She said, "No cornflakes."

Then my mother said, "Well, eat your egg," and she said, "No egg. Nasty egg." She said, "Nasty apple," too, and she spilled her milk all over the table. Wasn't she naughty?

My mother said, "You won't go to the Fair this afternoon if you don't eat it all up." So then my naughty little sister began to eat up her breakfast very quickly. She ate the cornflakes and the egg, but she really couldn't manage the apple, and my mother said, "Well, you ate most of your breakfast so I think we shall let you go to the Fair."

Shall I tell you why my naughty little sister hadn't wanted to eat her breakfast? *She was too excited.* And when my naughty little sister was excited, she was very cross and disobedient.

When the Fair-time came, my big cousin Jane came to fetch us. Then my naughty little sister got so excited that she was crosser than ever. My mother dressed her up in her new best blue dress and new best blue knickers, and her white shoes and blue socks, but my naughty little sister wouldn't help a bit. And you know what that means.

She went all stiff and stubborn, and she wouldn't put her arms in the arm-holes for herself,

and she wouldn't lift up her feet for her shoes,

and my mother said, "Very well, they shall go without you."

Then my naughty little sister lifted up her feet very quickly. Wasn't she bad?

We went on a bus to the Fair, and when we got there, it was very nice. We saw cows and horses and pigs and sheep and chickens, and lots and lots of people.

RACER

And there were big swings that went swingy-swing, swingy-swing, and roundabouts that went round and round, round and round. Then my naughty little sister said, "I want a swing! I want a swing!"

But my big cousin Jane said, "No, you are too little for those big swings, but you shall go on the little roundabout."

The little roundabout had wooden horses with real reins, and things to put your feet in, and there were little cars on the roundabout, and a little red fire-engine, and a little train.

First, we watched the roundabout going round and round, and when it went round all the cars and horses went up and down, up and down, and the fire-engine and the train went up and down too. The roundabout played music as it went round.

RAND
FLIERS

Then, when it stopped, my big cousin said, "Get on, both of you." There were lots of other children there, and some of them were afraid to go on the roundabout, but my little sister wasn't afraid. She was the first child to go on, and she got on all by herself, without *anyone* lifting her at all. Wasn't she a big girl?

And do you know what she did? She got into the seat of the red fire-engine, and rang and rang the bell. "Clonkle! Clonkle! Clonkle!" went the bell, and my little sister laughed and laughed, and when the roundabout went round it played nice music, and my naughty little sister said, "Hurrah. I'm going to put the fire out!"

My little sister had four rides on the roundabout. One, two, three, four rides. And then my big cousin Jane said, "We have spent all our money. We will go and look at the people buying horses."

But my little sister got thoroughly nasty again, and she said, "No horse. Nasty horses. Want roundabout." There, wasn't that bad of her? I'm glad you're not like that.

But my cousin said, "Come along at once," and my naughty little sister had to come, but do you know what she did, while we were looking at the horses? *She ran away.* I said she was a naughty child, you know.

Yes. She ran away, and we
couldn't find her anywhere.

We looked and looked. We
went to the roundabouts
and she wasn't there.

We went to the swings
and she wasn't there.

She wasn't at the pig place,

or the cow place

or the chicken place, or
any of the other places.

So then my big cousin Jane said, "We must ask a policeman. Because policemen are good to lost children."

We asked a lady if she could tell us where a policeman was, and the lady said, "Go over the road to the police-station."

So my cousin took me over the road to the police-station, and we went into a big door, and through another door, and we saw a policeman sitting without his hat on. And the policeman said, "How do you do, children. Can I help you?" Wasn't that nice of him?

Then my big cousin Jane said, "We have lost a naughty little girl." And she told the nice policeman all about my bad little sister, all about what her name was, and where we had lost her, and what she looked like, and the nice policeman wrote it all down in a big book.

Then the kind policeman said, "No, we haven't a little girl here, but if we find her, we will send her home to you in a big car."

So then my cousin Jane and I went home, and it was a long, long walk because we had spent all our pennies on the roundabout.

When we got home, what do you think? There was my naughty little sister, sitting at the table, eating her tea. She had got home before us after all. And do you know why that was? It was because a kind policeman had found her and taken her home in his big car.

And do you know, my naughty little sister said she'd never, never run off like that again, because it wasn't nice at all, being lost. She said it made her cry.

But, my naughty little sister said, if she did get lost again, she would find another nice policeman to take her home, because policemen are so kind to lost children.

First published in Great Britain 1952 in My Naughty Little Sister.
The edition first published 1979
by Methuen Children's Books Ltd, 11 New Fetter Lane, London EC4P 4EE
Reprinted 1981 and 1983
Paperback edition first published 1983
by Methuen Children's Books Ltd
Reprinted 1984

Printed in Great Britain by Blantyre Printing & Binding Co Ltd
ISBN 0 416 86840 1 (hardback)
ISBN 0 416 44570 5 (paperback)